P9-BZR-706

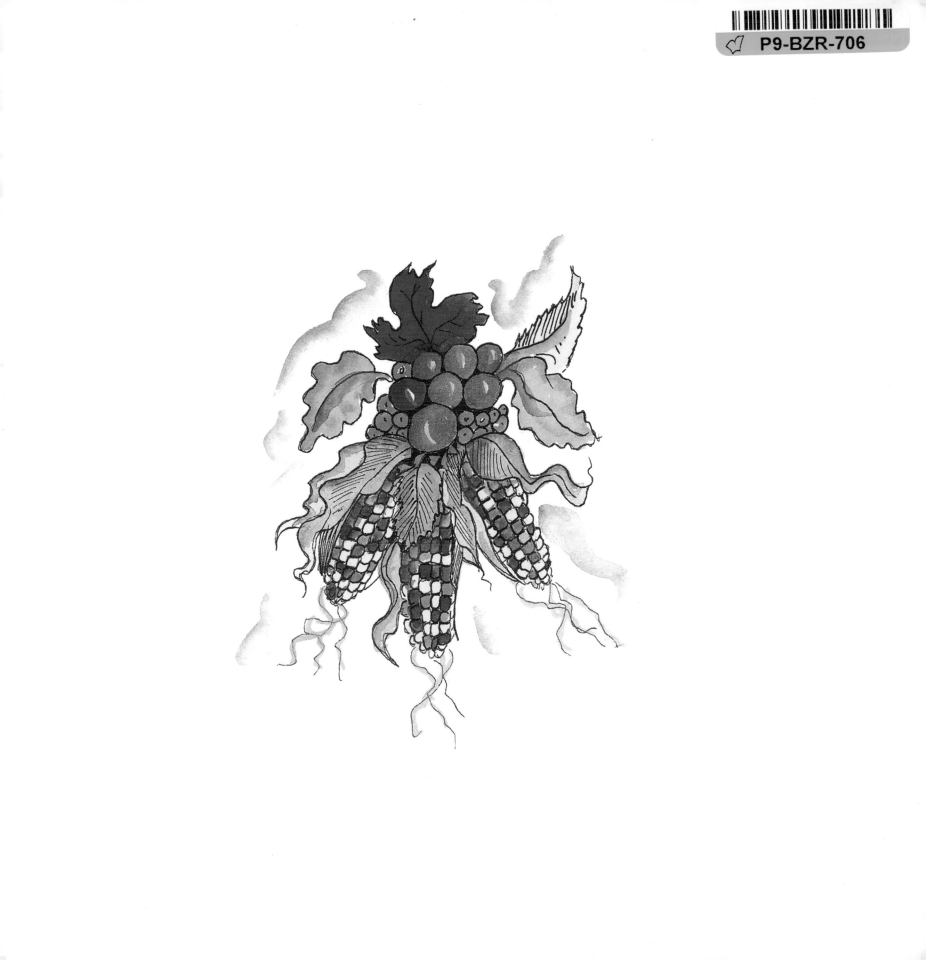

To all those who love
THANKSGIVING DAY

THANKSGIVING IS...

BY GAIL GIBBONS

Holiday House / New York

Copyright © 2004 by Gail Gibbons
All Rights Reserved
Printed in the United States of America
www.holidayhouse.com
5 7 9 10 8 6

Library of Congress Cataloging-in-Publication Data

Gibbons, Gail.
Thanksgiving is— / by Gail Gibbons—1st ed.
p. cm.
ISBN 0-8234-1849-9 (hardcover)
ISBN 0-8234-1979-7 (paperback)
1. Thanksgiving Day—Juvenile literature.
[1. Thanksgiving Day. 2. Holidays.] I. Title.

GT4975.G52 2004
394.2649—dc22
2003067645

ISBN-13: 978-0-8234-1849-7 (hardcover)
ISBN-13: 978-0-8234-1979-1 (paperback)

ISBN-10: 0-8234-1849-9 (hardcover)
ISBN-10: 0-8234-1979-7 (paperback)

THANKSGIVING IS...
A HOLIDAY FOR GIVING THANKS.

In the United States, Thanksgiving is celebrated on the fourth Thursday of November.

THANKSGIVING IS...
HARVEST CELEBRATIONS OF LONG AGO.

MIN

The Chinese baked moon cakes to celebrate a harvest.

Thousands of years ago, people had celebrations to give thanks for bountiful harvests. Egyptians praised their god Min, the god of plants and fertility. In China, the people honored the moon at harvesttime because it appeared to be at its brightest and perfectly round. They baked moon cakes to celebrate a harvest.

The Greeks worshiped their goddess of agriculture, Demeter (di·MEE·ter). The Romans' goddess of agriculture was named Ceres (SIR·eez). They offered the first foods from their harvest to her as thanks.

The ancient Jewish harvest festival, called Sukkot (soo·KOTE), was first celebrated thousands of years ago. Jews thanked God for his protection and for their food, as they still do today.

The MIDDLE AGES were from about 450 to about 1450.

During the Middle Ages, farmers in England held festivals to celebrate the end of the harvest.

THANKSGIVING IS...THE PILGRIMS.

In September 1620, a group of 101 passengers sailed from Plymouth, England, in search of a new home. These men, women, and children were called Pilgrims. They wanted the freedom to worship in their own way, which they had not been allowed to do.

They crossed the Atlantic Ocean on a small ship called the *Mayflower*. Their voyage was difficult. They sailed through many storms. One passenger died and a baby was born.

At last, after a long voyage, they came ashore at what is now Plymouth, Massachusetts.

The Pilgrims began to build homes. Winter came with its cold winds. The Pilgrims had little food to eat. Many of them died.

THANKSGIVING IS...NATIVE AMERICANS.

Two famous Indians who helped the settlers were SQUANTO (SKWAN·toe) and MASSASOIT (mass·uh·SOY·it).

When spring finally arrived, the Pilgrims were grateful. Indians taught them how to grow the foods that they themselves ate. Also they taught the Pilgrims how to be better hunters.

During the growing season, the crops grew and grew. The fall harvest was plentiful. The Pilgrims wanted to thank God for the abundance of food they would have for the coming winter.

There was a great feast. The Indians were invited. It was the Pilgrims' first Thanksgiving . . . the fall of 1621.

The first Thanksgiving lasted three days.

THANKSGIVING IS...A HOLIDAY.

In Canada, Thanksgiving is celebrated on the second Monday of October.

In 1863, President Abraham Lincoln proclaimed the last Thursday of November to be Thanksgiving Day. This was the first nationally declared Thanksgiving Day for the United States. Then in 1939, President Franklin Delano Roosevelt made a change and declared Thanksgiving Day to be the fourth Thursday of November.

THANKSGIVING HAS MANY SYMBOLS.
THERE ARE THANKSGIVING DECORATIONS.

In many ways, our Thanksgiving celebrations remind us of the Pilgrims' Thanksgiving. There are pumpkins, turkeys, fall leaves, and other symbols gathered together to look like harvesttime. Some homes are decorated.

THANKSGIVING IS... FAMILY AND FRIENDS.

Family and friends come together to share good times. It is time for loving and sharing.

THANKSGIVING IS...A THANKSGIVING FEAST!

Tables are filled with many of the same foods the Pilgrims shared with the Indians.

There is turkey, stuffing, cranberries . . .

sweet potatoes, beans, squash, cornbread, and other good things to eat.

THANKSGIVING IS...
THANKSGIVING DESSERTS, TOO.

There is pumpkin pie, mincemeat pie, bread pudding, baked apples . . . all kinds of treats.

THANKSGIVING IS...GIVING.

Sometimes people send Thanksgiving cards. They may give plants or flowers when they visit others.

THANKSGIVING IS...GAMES!

Families and friends may play outside . . . or go to a game.

THANKSGIVING IS... THANKSGIVING PLAYS.

There are plays about the Pilgrims and the Indians who helped them.

THANKSGIVING IS...PARADES!

There are floats, bands . . .

and big balloons.

THANKSGIVING IS...SHARING AND...

REMEMBERING OTHERS.

THANKSGIVING IS...
GIVING THANKS FOR MANY BLESSINGS.